Whispers in the dark.

lisa briggs

BookLeaf
Publishing

Presentation by *BookLeaf Publishing*

Web: www.bookleafpub.com

E-mail: info@bookleafpub.com

ISBN: 9789395621014

First edition 2022

DEDICATION

I am dedicated to my writing and my work.

ACKNOWLEDGEMENT

I acknowledge this is my work.

PREFACE

Sad poems happy poems and all kinds of poems

Blue bird

Fluttering blue bird

Flapping its wings in the wind

Fluttering blue bird.

The cold

Dont leave me out in the cold for I am already old, there is battle wounds and scars if you only knew of the stories that I told.

I'm scared I wont wake up, I'm scared that my cup will overflow and not grow.

So please dont leave me out in the cold.

Warriors dont quit

Anxiety is like a sickness you cant escape but you keep showing up.

You keep pushing and you keep striving cause what else can you do, warriors dont quit, they get back up and they fight until they cant no more that's a true warrior

Life is scary and living with anxiety is a battle but as they say the only way is through right?.

Scared

I dont know who I am anymore slowly losing
my identity slowly into the abyss.
Wondering if I will ever return ,

Lost and alone as my soul trys to heal I dont
know if I ever will.

I'm emotional

5

I'm emotional and I'm raw,
I cry alot
I open up and close up I make up and I stuff up,
But yes it's what I'm going through and I'm sorry
for that.

I dont feel worth it I dont feel like I'm wanted
and I'm not perfect,
I am lost and still need to find myself but while
I'm finding myself I still want you by my side if
that's okay?

Dont lose hope

Am I wrong or am I right?
Will i get some sleep tonight
My mind is racing most of the time i get no
peace sometimes the only peace is when I'm
asleep.

Just wanting some help and a way out of this
clouded by the jokes and all the mist .

A Monster inside

How can you love me when I dont love myself.

Theres alot to love but I cant see it.
I look in the mirror and see an empty shell.

I'm trying to find my way out of the madness out
of the Sadness and out of the pain.

But it's hard.

I want to be with you I really do but I keep
pushing the people I love away most .

Maybe I am a monster that no one would want
to come near.

A devil in disguise?

Please dont leave me I need you here.
This isnt who I am clouded by my perception of
who I really am

Deep inside I'm nice you will see.

I'm drowning

I'm in slow motion I'm trapped.

I'm drowning

I cant breath.

I'm under water deeply immersed in the sea.

I'm not looking for a saviour
Because the only person who can save me is me.

Just leave me alone

Trying to find the light
When I'm brought down its hard.

I wish you could stop cant you see I'm worn
down

Cant you see I can't make a sound.

Trying to find the light.

What is fear?

What is fear?

Fear is a liar.
Face everything and rise.

We need to rise
Rise above our thoughts
That swirl inside our brain.

It's only fear breath it in and let it go.

Your going to be alright.

They are only thoughts

These thoughts are wild
The sad and the bad makes me shake makes my
mind quake.

For goodness sake just leave me alone so I can
breath away the pain and stay safe these
thoughts are wild.

We live in an illusion

We live in an illusion
We live a lie.

Theres a fine line between sanity and losing
your sanity.

My mind is racing a million thoughts at once

I keep dieng and keep coming back to life but
I'm so tired of these lies my own head tells me
why cant everything be okay?.

Why does everything has to be so messed up .
When will this end?

Anxiety

Anxiety is a word that cripples you.

Takes away your breathing rhythm.

Trying to catch a breath.

The past haunts you and nightmares are
protruding in your brain all this pain

This is anxiety.

My palms are sweaty my knees are weak this is
anxiety.

Breath

We are only human we are not immortal.
We have feelings we ahve emotions and hearts
and souls.

We are only who we are

We think our ways out of situations transcending
in this space and time

Elements under our skin.

So take a deep breath and realise we are only
human and that's more than okay.

A dog called shadow

A dog called shadow is such a joy to be around she follows me wherever I go.

She has a waggy tail and is very big with a personality that is hyperactive and fun. She sits out in the sun all day but doesn't let it burn her she is a dog called shadow.

My nephew

My nephew is only five but he is the best thing that's happened to me such a kid and we have so much fun he is my nephew and I love him.

He has a massive personality and a huge smile he brings me lots of joy he is full of love and isnt rarely a naughty boy .

The sun

The sun is breaking through the stain glassed window it is only six am.

I look outside and can see all my friends they wave hello and I smile and say the sun is shinging today but the sun wont go away and I'm hoping it won't because I do not like cloudy days.

My heart beats like a drum

My heart beats like a drum when ever your near we have been together now for four years .

Think of all the cheers and the beers and the laughter and the tears I'm glad I met you because you make my life happier and joyful and no fears.

www.ingramcontent.com/pod-product-compliance
Lightning Source LLC
Chambersburg PA
CBHW061327140726
47998CB00007B/2578